Town of Tiny Hope

By
Karol King

To Kate, Caroline, Grace, and Nora

The town of Tiny Hope was a little village that sat on the edge of a very wide, very blue river. The river was so wide that in some places it looked like a lake. But it was not a lake, and its waters flowed clear down into the ocean.

Tiny Hope seems like a strange name for a town, don't you think? Nobody could remember for sure why it had been named that. Mrs. Bumblebee Purple Blue Pot said that one of her ancestors way back, was a founding father—that means that he was one of the first people to live in the town and helped make the buildings and the streets.

Anyway, she said that her ancestor gave it the name "Tiny Hope" because he said that he had a "tiny hope" that someday this little town would become a great city. Well, it did not become a great city and instead stayed a small town.

But Mr. Carnation Pork Belly Lancaster said that no, it wasn't like that at all. He said that his great-great-great-great-great Aunt Hope was the first baby born in the town many, many years ago. He said that the town was named after her, and since she was a newborn baby (and as we all know, newborn babies are usually pretty tiny), they called her (and the town) "Tiny Hope."

Well, however it got its name, Tiny Hope was a beautiful little town that had interesting people and pretty little houses in it.

This book tells the stories of some things that happened to the people who lived in the town of Tiny Hope.

Some of the people's names were pretty strange; so the next few pages show pictures of their names to help you remember who they were.

Mrs. Bumblebee Purple Blue Pot

Chip or Chips

Mr. Testy Temper Hot Rod Titmouse

Pickle Partner Pondering Porpoise

Mr. Lester the Lordly Lion

Mrs. Ice Cream Sandwich Browning Frog

Orange Pumpkin Dandelion House

Mr. Carnation Pork Belly Lancaster

Mrs. Mouse and her Five Babies

First Story

One day Chip, (or Chips) Purple Blue Pot went down to the river to play. We need to stop right here and talk about Chip's name. Was his name Chip, or Chips? He didn't know for sure. He really **wanted** to know, but when he would ask his mother, Mrs. Bumblebee Purple Blue Pot, she would say that she honestly could not remember whether she had named him Chip or Chips.

"Well," Chip (or Chips) would say back to her, "Now, Mother, if you really loved me and cared for me, you would try to find my BC (birth certificate) that would say for sure whether my name is Chip or Chips."

But today she replied, "Now, Chip, you know that I love you, but I am just starting to make a blueberry pie for Mr. Carnation Pork Belly Lancaster, and I can't stop right in the middle of making the pie dough, because my hands are all greasy and full of flour. Surely you can see that for yourself, and she sighed loudly and waved her hands in front of his face.

"Mother," he said back a little too loudly, "You must have named me Chip, because I'm just one boy, not two; so how could you possibly have named me Chips?"

And she would say, "You know, Chips, I think I named you Chips, because I always thought I would have twins sometime, and since it didn't work out that way, I decided to call you Chips instead of Chip just to help me remember that I once thought about having twins."

There were certain things that Chip (or Chips) could just **never** understand about his mother! But that's not what this story is really about. It's about when Chip (or Chips) went down to the big, beautiful river to play with the sand and the stones, and the wonderful thing that happened that day.

He had just finished building a crooked little tower of stones, when he looked up and saw something dark and rather large moving in the water. It was too far away for him to see for sure what it was; so he ran over to the pier that stretched out into the blue water and watched as the dark thing turned to swim towards him.

Suddenly, a beautiful gray head rose out of the deep blueness very close to him and looked at him with its great brown eyes. It was a dolphin—well, some people would call it a porpoise. Again, that's the trouble with names. Some people say one thing and some people another. As a matter of fact, this porpoise's name was Pickle Partner Pondering Porpoise, but Chip did not know that yet. Anyway—Chip was so surprised and excited to see this beautiful animal that he just flopped down on his stomach at the edge of the pier and put out his hand to stroke its head. And what do you think? The porpoise smiled and smiled at him.

And then Chips said, "Oh, my gorgeous friend, what is your name?" But almost immediately, he wished he had not said that, as the porpoise looked at him with very sad eyes, and stuttered, "M-m-m-y n-n-na-a-me   is P-P-P.... We-l-l-l-l-l, it's P-P-P-P...," and to Chip's amazement, the porpoise started to cry. Two big tears ran down his sleek, wet face and fell into the river water.

At first Chips did not know what to do or to say. He just looked at the porpoise and he sort of wanted to laugh, because it sounded so funny to hear the porpoise stuttering and blowing water out of his mouth, when he tried to talk. But he did **not** laugh. Even though his mother, Mrs. Bumblebee Purple Blue Pot, was a very busy lady and did not have time to look up his real name, she **had** taught him to be polite and respectful to other people and to never, ever laugh at them and make them feel uncomfortable.

What should he say to his new friend? Should he pat his head again and smile at him? Should he jump into the water and swim with him? But he didn't have time to think long, because the porpoise suddenly dived very deep into the water and came up many yards away, but this time he was singing!

And here is what he sang: "My name is Pickle Partner Pondering Porpoise, and I can sing and sing and sing." Again and again he dived down into the water and came up singing his name: "My name is Pickle Partner Pondering Porpoise, and how I love to sing! I cannot talk, but I can sing and sing and sing!!"

Chips was so amazed that he sat up quickly and held his knees close to his chest, as though he were hugging his knees. Actually, he was thinking how much he would love to hug the porpoise.

Just then another wonderful thing happened. Mr. Testy Temper Hot Rod Titmouse, who was sitting on a high branch in a tree close by, said loudly, "OMG! That is the most beautiful song I have ever heard! Everybody in the world and in the ocean and in the rivers and the ponds and the cities and on the farms and in the woods should hear that gorgeous song! Sing it again Porpoise! Sing it again!"

Now, the reason this part of the story is so surprising is that Mr. Testy Temper Hot Rod Titmouse **never, ever** had anything nice to say about other birds or people or things. When anyone would talk to him, he would look angry and say crossly, "How disgusting!" That is just plain baloney!" "Why are people so schtupid??!! (He said it like that--"schtupid," instead of "stupid" the way most of us say it here in America.) Chip (or Chips) thought he might just fall over with surprise to hear something positive come out of Mr. Testy Temper Hot Rod Titmouse's mouth!

"This is a day that will go down in history," Chip thought to himself."

And you know, it sort of did go down in history, because it seemed to Chips that the porpoise's song came around in a full circle and then went out again to the waves and then back again to shore so that even the dogs and the cats, the birds and the people in Tiny Hope heard that wonderful song. Over and over and over the song went spiraling upward to the blue, blue sky and white fluffy clouds and then back down again to the green grass and pink and yellow and purple and red flowers and to the red and gray bricks in the Town Square.

Even Mr. Lester the Lordly Lion, who was walking down towards the Town Square right at that moment, exclaimed, "Wow! Why I'm not sure even I could sing a song like that! What a beautiful, wonderful song! I love it! Sing it again, Porpoise!"

Now, Mr. Lester the Lordly Lion walked with a cane and had sort of thin, brownish hair. That was fine, but the problem was that he felt superior to everybody else, looked down on his friends and neighbors, and was mainly an unhappy person. Before he moved to Tiny Hope, he had had no hope at all that he could ever be happy, but when he heard about the Town of Tiny Hope, he decided to move there, "For he said, "Tiny Hope is better than no hope at all!" And he was so right!

And then Mrs. Ice Cream Sandwich Browning Frog, who lived in a huge, gorgeous mansion where they had parties all the time and many servants and people to help out, decided to have the grandest party she had ever had yet. Why, she didn't know for sure, but she just knew that it was the right time for such a party!

And at Orange Pumpkin Dandelion House, where the Mouse Family lived, there was so much warmth and coziness that Mrs. Mouse wondered why she could **not** keep from smiling and singing to herself and to her babies. It's true that she had just finished crocheting five tiny blankets for her five itty-bitty pink babies, and she was happy about that, but there was something more going on--she could tell! To be totally honest, most of the time she usually felt a little sad and embarrassed that they were so poor and had to live in the rickety desk drawer down in Mr. Carnation Pork Belly Lancaster's basement. (That's who owned the Orange Pumpkin Dandelion House.) Still, it was **somewhere** to live and that was more than some people (and mice) could say! But today—today she just felt so happy!

Orange Pumpkin Dandelion House

Now, why that house was named Orange Pumpkin Dandelion House was more than anyone could ever figure out. Maybe way back in time, it had been painted orange; it sort of looked that way, but it definitely was **not** shaped like a pumpkin. As far as dandelions, well, in the early springtime, Mr. Carnation Pork Belly Lancaster's yard was **full** of bright yellow dandelions that glowed like a million little suns in the universe. So, I guess that's where the dandelion part of the name came from.

Chip (or Chips) decided that the reason the porpoise that Pickle Partner Pondering Porpoise came by that day was to tell everybody in Tiny Hope to sing, sing, sing! Sing your name! Sing your song, and maybe it will make even Mr. Testy Temper Hot Rod Titmouse happy! And **that** is **something!!!**

Mrs. Ice Cream Sandwich Browning Frog's Huge Party House

Second Story

After Mrs. Bumblebee Purple Blue Pot's children were grown and had left home, Mrs. BPBP decided that she wanted to move to a big city. She loved the streets and lights, and the hustle-bustle of people coming and going all hours of the day and night. She liked the urban noises—people talking, sirens screaming, and horns honking. Those sights and sounds made her feel alive and happy.

She loved living there with people close all around her. She liked to look down from her windows high up in the apartment building, at the people walking down the street. What were they doing out there? Why were they walking so quickly? Or, if she saw two or three people standing talking together, she would wonder what they were talking about. She almost never felt lonely when she was in the city.

There were interesting old buildings and beautiful parks very close to her building. She loved to see the lovely spring flowers, and in the fall, she admired all the gorgeous, colored leaves falling slowly from the trees. And in the winter, there was the lovely white snow, piled high and gleaming in the light from the street lamps.

However, even though Mrs. Bumblebee PBP was very happy living in the city, she missed her friends in the town of Tiny Hope, especially Mrs. Mouse. Now, Mrs. Mouse was much younger than Mrs. Bumblebee, and she had very young children to take care of; so she could not move to the city. Once in a while, Mrs. Bumblebee would take the bus out into the country and visit her friends in Tiny Hope Town. Those were always happy days, when she could see her old friends and laugh and talk with them.

Then one day, Mrs. Bumblebee had an idea. She bought a little camera that she could easily carry in her hand or in her pocket, and she would walk about the streets taking pictures of the things she loved. Then she would send them to Mrs. Mouse and write her stories of things that happened to her.

First of all—here are some of the pictures that she sent to Mrs. Mouse.

Look at all the colors!

Here is fruit market out on the street.

Two Beautiful Restaurants Downtown

One night she saw a man with a bright yellow car.

Another day she saw horses pulling a long cart with people in it.

There were pink and purple houses.

People Singing and Playing Instruments in a Café

A Girl with a Funny Mask

A University with Beautiful Buildings

A Statue of a President

An Apartment Balcony with Animal Figures

Christmas Bears

Tall Buildings Pointing High up in the Air with a Crack of Sky Between

Red Buildings and Blue and Red Motorcycles

A Green Building and Blue Sky

And a Bright Red Bus

A Blue House

One Man and a Room Full of Books

The City in the Daytime

The City at Night

And now here is one of the stories that Mrs. Bumblebee Purple Blue Pot wrote to Mrs. Mouse.

This one happened in the wintertime. One late afternoon, Mrs. Bumblebee took the bus up a very steep hill several blocks from her house so that she could go to school at the big university at the top of the hill. Mrs. Bumblebee loved to read and to go to school; so she had a great time in class that night, but what a surprise awaited her when she stepped outside of the building and onto the street!

During class, a huge snowstorm had come through the city. In fact, it was still snowing when she walked outside. Very slowly, she walked towards the bus stop; then she saw something that was pretty discouraging—the bus was just sitting at the side of the street and was not going anywhere. She opened the door and spoke to the bus driver:

"When will you be going back downtown?" she asked.

"Oh, Ma'am," he replied, "This bus is not moving until the streets are cleared. There is ice underneath the snow, and it is way too dangerous for us to try to drive in this kind of weather." v

"Well, what shall I do? How shall I get home?" Mrs. Bumblebee asked with a worried frown on her face.

The bus driver just shrugged his shoulders and said, "Ma'am, I don't know what to tell you, but I will say again, 'This bus is not moving until the streets are in better shape.'"

Mrs. Bumblebee stepped back down out of the bus doorway and stood for a moment thinking. She wound her scarf very tightly around her head, pulled her gloves up above her wrists, and said to herself, "Well, I'm not staying here all night! I'm going to try to make it down the hill on my own."

So off she started, walking very, very slowly; in fact, she did not even lift her feet off the ice and snow. She just shuffled along, trying not to fall down. There were cars parked along the sides of the street; so she tried to hold onto them, but they were not much help, because they were covered with ice and were very slick. Even though it was a dark night, there were street lights on with their golden light streaming down upon the sidewalk. So she could see all right, but she could not walk quickly, the way she usually did.

Snow in the Park

She got to the corner where the street turned sharply to the left and then became very steep—down, down it went many blocks down to the bottom of the hill. Just then, she noticed a group of young people standing in the shadow of a big brick wall on the other side of the street. They were laughing and talking—maybe about the weather, who knows? It <u>was</u> exciting to be out with so much danger all around!

Then suddenly—Oh no! Oops! Oh no! She was going to fall! Her feet were sliding!! She grabbed onto a car door handle as hard as she could, but her feet were still

slipping and sliding under her. She was going to slide right underneath the car! What was she going to do?? She wanted to cry for help, but who would hear her?

Just then, out of the darkness came a strong voice, "Here, Ma'am. Hold onto me. I'll help you down the hill." What a wonderful surprise! Who had come to rescue her? She looked up into the face of a kind young man. Evidently, he had left his group of friends and was coming to help her! He bent his arm, and she stuck her hand into the crook of his arm, and very, very slowly together they made their way down that icy hill. It took several minutes, but they were good minutes. She felt so safe and happy with the young man.

"You know," she said, suddenly looking up at him. "I think you are an angel!" They both smiled at each other. But he shook his dark head vigorously and said, "Oh no, Ma'am. I wish I were an angel, but I'm not! Not at all!"

"Well, you never know," she replied. "Maybe you are, but you just don't know it!" Again, they both laughed. He held her arm tightly until they finally reached level ground, and she felt that she could make it on home alone. They stopped walking, and for a minute, they both looked at each other.

"Goodbye and thank you so much!" Mrs. Bumblebee Purple Blue Pot said, and she held his hand tightly for a moment longer. Then she started off for home, and he turned around and walked back up the hill to his friends. What a wonderful, magical night!

Third Story

At the Farm

One day after coming back from riding the bus, Mrs. Bumblebee found a letter in her mailbox. It was from her dear friend, Mrs. Mouse, who lived in the village of Tiny Hope. Mrs. Bumblebee was SO happy to get the letter that she just sat right down on a kitchen chair and read it even before she took off her coat and put her groceries away. Here is what she read:

"Dear Friend Bumblebee,

I have quite a story to tell you! You remember my five babies, Mary, Elizabeth, Ellen, Rose, and Charlie. How they have grown since you left Tiny Hope! They are getting to be so big and running around all over the place. I try to keep them close to the house, but Charlie, especially, loves to get outside the fence and go explore the world.

Well, what an adventure he had yesterday! He left the village, climbed through a fence at the edge of a big farm, wiggled through a little hole in the house, and got right into the people's kitchen. He had never seen anything like this before. I'm sure his tiny wet nose wiggled and jiggled when he smelled all the wonderful smells in there.

Mrs. Farmer Wife had been baking pies for her family, and the smells were so wonderful! For a long time, he sat quietly in one corner of the cupboard just enjoying all those wonderful smells. He thinks that maybe he even went to sleep in one corner of a drawer in which Mrs. Farmer Wife kept her sugar and flour. It was warm and comfortable in there!

The Farm House

When he finally woke up, he heard different voices from the one he had heard from Mrs. Farmer Wife. Actually, she had been singing while she was making the pies, but he had also heard her talking on the phone to one of her friends too; so when he heard these voices, he was sure that some other people had come into the kitchen, and Mrs. Farmer Wife wasn't there anymore.

Very quietly and cautiously, he crept over to a place where he saw light coming into the drawer. Putting his eye up to the light, he peered out and saw two girls working in the kitchen. They were clearing off the table from supper; then they began to wash and dry the dishes. They were laughing and talking and telling each other stories.

Washing Dishes

And then—suddenly, right behind him, he smelled the most delicious smell of his whole life! Oh my goodness! What could it be?! It was very different from the wonderful pies he had smelled. His nose wrinkled and twitched. He could not get enough of this delightful aroma! Whatever could it be? Cautiously, he looked around, and then he saw something he had never seen before.

There was a tiny room, at least that is what it looked like to him, and inside of it was a yellow square, and…that is where this delicious smell was coming from. His mouth started to water. He just HAD to taste that yellow square. It smelled so good. Just imagine what it would taste like! He was positive that it would taste much better than the grass, clover, and flower seeds that he usually ate.

So, without once thinking of danger, he stepped up on the little step and right into that little room towards that wonderful smell, when…whack! Something sharp hit his neck. Ouch! Oh no! He couldn't move! He had wanted to taste that wonderful smell, and now he could not move his head. He thrashed his paws all around.

"Let me go! Let me go!" he squeaked as loudly as he could. "Mama, Mama," he called. "Help! Help!"

Just then, it got very bright all around him. One of the girls had opened the door to the cupboard.

"Come here, Elsie," she cried. "Come here! There is the cutest little mouse caught in the trap with the cheese."

Cheese! Oh, that was the name of that wonderful smell! Cheese! What a funny name for something that smelled so wonderful.

Again, he squeaked and squeaked, "Help! Help! Please, please help me!" He was starting not to be able to breathe, and it felt as though his eyes were going to pop out of his head, because of the pressure on his neck.

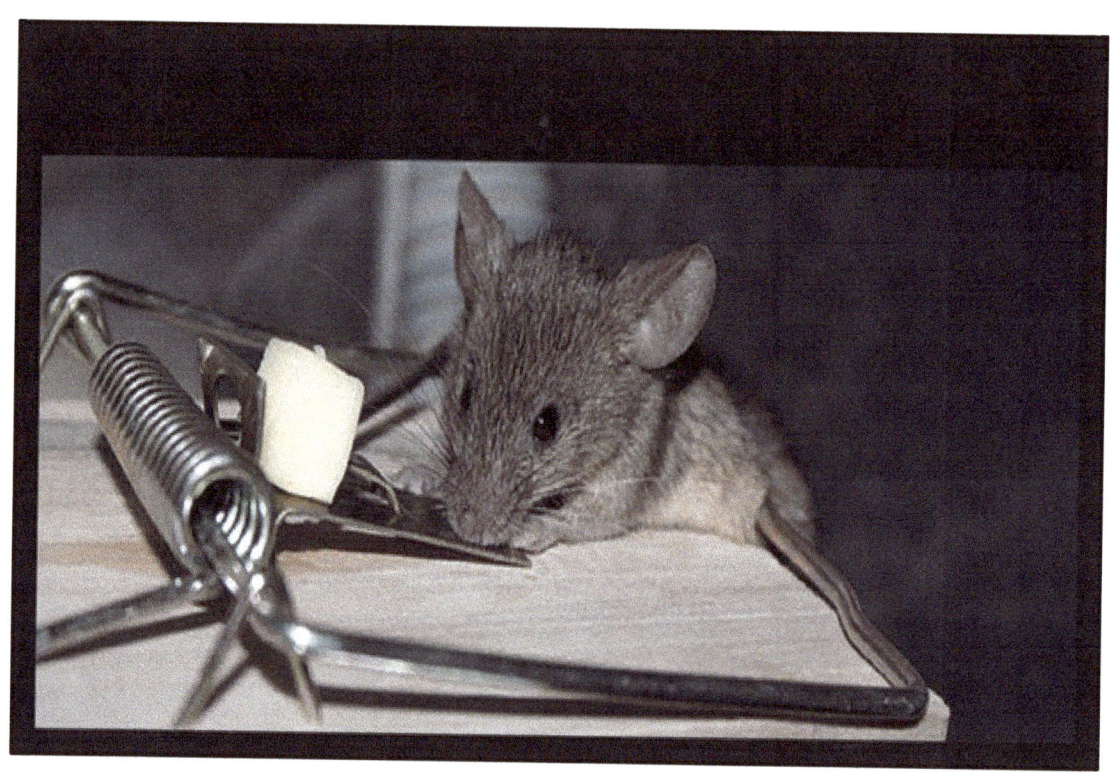

Charlie in the Trap

"Oh, Lisa," said Elsie, he is SO cute! Look at his shiny, sparkly eyes! We can NOT let him die!"

Both Elsie and Lisa looked at each other. What should they do? They knew that Mother did not want mice in the house, but they just could NOT let this beautiful little mouse baby die!

And then just as quick as a wink, Lisa, reached down, picked up the trap with the cheese and the baby mouse in it. Both Lisa and Elsie ran as fast as they could out the kitchen door, down the back steps, across the green grass, up the steps of the stile, and into the big clover field.

They knelt down and lifted the cruel metal bar from Charlie's neck. He was free! He was free! He looked at the girls with his shiny, bright eyes.

58

"Thank you! Thank you!" he said excitedly. Then quick as a wink, he ran through the clover and back to his home—to his mother and sisters.

Lisa and Elsie climbed back over the stile and walked back to the house. They were a little worried. What would Mother say about their letting the little mouse go? Oh well, it was done now. They could not get the little mouse back! Actually, they were very glad that they could not.

This is a stile, which is a double ladder to climb over a fence.

Later that evening, when all the dishes were done and everything was nice and tidy in the house, and they were sitting in the living room together, Elsie said, "Mama, we have something to tell you."

"What is that?" Mother asked, looking at them curiously.

"Well, while we were doing dishes, we heard a snap and then a 'Squeak! Squeak!' So we looked inside the cupboard, and there was a darling little baby mouse with bright, shiny eyes caught in the trap and looking up at us." Elsie stopped speaking and looked over at Lisa.

"Uh, and…so…we picked up the trap with the baby mouse in it, and we took him back to the field so that he could be free," said Lisa.

Mother shook her head. "Why do you think I set that trap in the cupboard?" she asked. "I don't want mice in our house, eating our food and making a mess all over the place. Now, that little mouse will grow up to be a big mouse and will come back here, and goodness only knows what he will think up to eat!" She shook her head, and yet both girls saw a little smile around the corners of her mouth.

Well, at least she didn't seem too angry at them. That was good!

But just before she put them to bed that night, Mother said, "Don't you ever let another mouse of a mousetrap in this house." And they never did, because they never saw another mouse in the kitchen.

The Farmer and His Family

Riding the Tractor on the Farm